From A to Z, a world of careers so wide,
where children like you can freely decide.

A is for Astronaut,
exploring the skies so far,

Astronauts are brave explorers! They go on exciting adventures beyond Earth to places like the Moon and outer space. They get to fly rocket ships, float in space, and wear cool space suits.

B is for Baker,
making pastries and cookies, you'll be a star.

Did you know that bakers are like kitchen scientists? They use special ingredients like yeast to make bread rise and turn into those fluffy, yummy loaves we love to eat.

C is for Chef,

creating dishes, delicious and grand,

Chefs are culinary artists! They create amazing dishes using their imagination and special ingredients. Some chefs even wear tall white hats called 'toques' to show they're the boss in the kitchen.

D is for Doctor,
healing with care, lending a helping hand.

Doctors help us heal when we feel unwell! They use special tools like stethoscopes to listen to our hearts and help us stay healthy; they're like real-life superheroes for your health!

E is for Engineer,
building things, both big and small,

Engineers are problem-solving wizards! They design and build things like bridges and even the tallest skyscrapers. They use math and science to create amazing structures that make our world a better place to live.

F is for Firefighter,
brave, always ready to answer the call.

Firefighters are everyday heroes! When there's a fire or an emergency, they rush in to save the day. They even have special suits and equipment to keep them safe while helping others.

G is for
Graphic Designer,
bringing art to the screen,

Graphic designers are artists in the digital world! They create amazing pictures and designs on computers. These designs can be in books, video games, and even greeting cards.

H is for
Historian,
Studying the past they've never seen.

Historians are like time travellers! They study the past and help us learn about how people lived a long, long time ago. They look at ancient maps and explore forgotten cities to unlock the secrets of history.

I is for Illustrator,
drawing with colours and grace,

Illustrators tell stories with pictures! They draw amazing images you see in books and magazines which help make the stories come to life. Every time you open a book, you're entering a world of wonder and imagination.

J is for Journalist,
writing stories, from every place.

Journalists inform the public about what is going on in the world. They cover a wide range of events, searching for stories to write about, from fun events to important world-wide discoveries.

K is for
K-9 Handler,
working with dogs so smart,

K-9 handlers work with specially trained dogs who are very clever and can sniff out important items, catch criminals, and help the police solve mysteries. It's like having furry detectives on the case!

L is for Librarian,
sharing books, where stories start.

Librarians take care of all the wonderful books in the library and help us find the perfect stories to read. They also help people find information using computers and the Internet.

M is for Marine Biologist,
diving in the deep blue sea,

Marine biologists are underwater scientists! They dive into the deep sea to study all the incredible creatures that live there, like colourful fish, dolphins, and even gigantic whales.

N is for

Nurse,
caring for patients, with love and glee.

Nurses are like superheroes in the hospital! They take care of people when they're not feeling well, and they always have a kind smile to share. Nurses make sure that everyone feels better, and they're always ready to help.

O is for
Ornithologists,
watching birds in the air,

Ornithologists are experts on birds! They observe and study various bird species in their natural habitat, including where birds migrate and how they make their nests.

P is for Palaeontologist,
finding fossils that are rare.

Palaeontologists are the ultimate dinosaur detectives! They dig up and study prehistoric plants, animals, and fossils that existed millions of years ago.

Q is for
Quantum Physicist,
exploring the tiny and vast,

Quantum physicists are explorers of the tiniest things! They study the smallest particles in the universe, like electrons and quarks. Quantum physicists help us understand the amazing secrets of the microscopic world!

R is for Robotics Engineer,
creating robots that last.

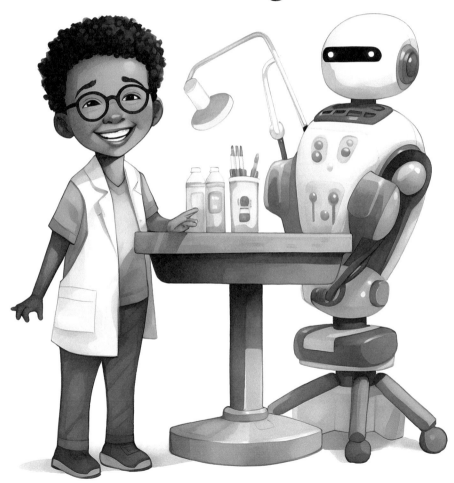

Robotics engineers are the creators of robot friends! They design and build all kinds of robots, from ones that vacuum your house to ones that explore other planets.

S is for Scientist,
experiments they pursue,

Scientists are explorers of the unknown! They ask questions, conduct experiments, and make incredible discoveries. They study everything, from how plants grow to the mysteries of the universe.

T is for Teacher,
inspire learning, and that's what they do.

Teachers are guides on your learning adventure! They help you discover new things and teach you about the world. They inspire, motivate, encourage, and educate, making sure you grow smarter every day.

U is for
Urban Planner,
designing cities with care,

Urban planners are city puzzle solvers! They design and organise cities to make them better places to live. They decide where roads, parks, and buildings should go.

♥

V is for
Veterinarian,
for animals, they are always there.

Veterinarians are animal doctors! They take care of all our furry and feathered friends, from cats and dogs to elephants and eagles. They make sure all animals are strong and healthy, like your doctor does for you!

W is for Welder,
welding into the night,

Welders are like modern-day blacksmiths! They use a special tool called a welding machine to join pieces of metal together by melting them and fusing them into strong and sturdy objects like fences and gates.

X is for
X-ray Technician,
bring health in sight.

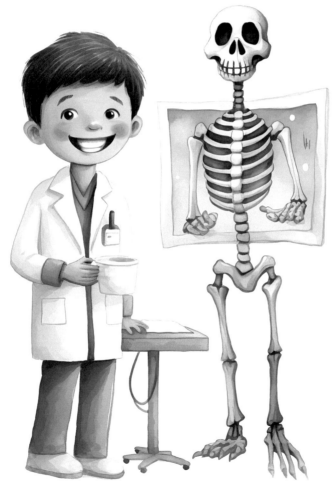

X-ray technicians are like secret agents with a special camera! They use X-rays to take pictures inside your body to help doctors see what's going on with your skeleton.

♥

Y is for YouTube Creator,
sharing talents galore,

YouTube creators are storytellers of the internet! They make fun and exciting videos about things they love, from games and toys to adventures, science and cooking. It's like having your very own TV show on the internet.

Z is for Zookeeper,
caring for animals they adore.

Zookeepers are animal caretakers! They take care of all the majestic creatures in the zoo, from giraffes to birds. They make sure the animals have yummy food, comfy homes, and lots of fun things to do.

Astronaut

Baker

Chef

Doctor

Illustrator

Journalist

K-9 Handler

Librarian

Quantum Physicist

Robotics Engineer

Scientist

Teacher

YouTube Creator

Zookeeper

Engineer

Firefighter

Graphic Designer

Historian

Marine Biologist

Nurse

Ornithologist

Paleontologist

Urban Planner

Veterinarian

Welder

X-ray Technician

So kids, dream big, explore, and play, in the world
of careers, you'll find your own way.

Aim for the stars, let your imagination soar, the world's
full of wonders, just waiting to explore.

With passion and hard work, you'll reach great heights,
in the A to Z of careers, your future's so bright!

Made in United States
Troutdale, OR
04/19/2024

19308878R00019